# Stencil Art

# ART COLORING BOOK

# Harry Potter

## AND THE CHAMBER OF SECRETS

With Stencils

SCHOLASTIC INC.

New York  Toronto  London  Auckland  Sydney
Mexico City  New Delhi  Hong Kong  Buenos Aires

ISBN 0-439-41897-6

12 11 10 9 8 7 6 5 4 3 2     2 3 4 5 6 7/0

Book design by Joan Moloney
Illustrations by Aristides Ruiz

Printed in the U.S.A.

First printing, October 2002